P9-DOG-483

PLASTIC, AHOY!

INVESTIGATING THE
GREAT PACIFIC GARBAGE PATCH

PATRICIA **NEWMAN**   PHOTOGRAPHS BY ANNIE **CRAWLEY**

Ⅲ MILLBROOK PRESS / MINNEAPOLIS

TO ELISE AND
SCOTT —P.N.

HR, RA, CP, PP,
LR, TK, MB,
WN, RP, HP, PK
& ALL OCEAN
PROTECTORS —A.C.

Top: A dip net catches plastic off the side of *New Horizon.*

Bottom: The SEAPLEX team rescued Lucky the dog from an ocean net.

Facing page: Velella velella jellies are beautiful and fun to say, too!

Text copyright © 2014 by Patricia Newman
Photographs copyright © 2014 by Annie Crawley

All rights reserved. International copyright secured. No part of this book may be reproduced, stored in a retrieval system, or transmitted in any form or by any means—electronic, mechanical, photocopying, recording, or otherwise—without the prior written permission of Lerner Publishing Group, Inc., except for the inclusion of brief quotations in an acknowledged review.

Millbrook Press
A division of Lerner Publishing Group, Inc.
241 First Avenue North
Minneapolis, MN 55401 USA

For reading levels and more information, look up this title at www.lernerbooks.com.

Library of Congress Cataloging-in-Publication Data

Newman, Patricia.
    Plastic, ahoy! : investigating the great Pacific garbage patch / by Patricia Newman.
      pages   cm
    Includes index.
    ISBN 978–1–4677–1283–5 (lib. bdg. : alk. paper)
    ISBN 978–1–4677–2541–5 (EB pdf)
    1. Marine pollution—Juvenile literature. 2. Marine pollution—Pacific Ocean. 3. Plastic marine debris—Environmental aspects—Juvenile literature. 4. Plastic scrap—Environmental aspects—Juvenile literature. 5. Waste disposal in the ocean. I. Title.
    GC1090.N48 2014
    363.738—dc23   2013017773

Manufactured in the United States of America
5-44473-13185-6/23/2017

C✦NTENTS

PERMISSION TO COME ABOARD, CAPTAIN?

DARCY

CHELSEA

MIRIAM

MIRIAM GOLDSTEIN, CHELSEA ROCHMAN, AND DARCY TANIGUCHI were going to sea. A mystery awaited them in the middle of the Pacific Ocean. Several tons of plastic floated in the water. The plastic had drifted there from around the world. It killed birds and marine life that ate it. Miriam, Chelsea, and Darcy studied the ocean in graduate school. They knew only a little about the ocean dump. They were more worried about what they didn't know.

Scientists thought that large amounts of plastic in the water might affect the way ocean life grows and develops. Eventually it might even harm the wider ocean, Earth's oxygen supply, and people—the ones who created the mess. But they didn't know for sure. No one had studied the floating plastic before.

Miriam, Chelsea, and Darcy decided to be some of the first. For three weeks, they would live and work on a small research ship. They charted a course to sail more than 1,000 miles (1,610 kilometers) into open water. Despite ocean swells and cramped living quarters, they would work twelve-hour shifts observing and collecting ocean plastic. They planned to study their samples and experiment to learn more.

They hoped to begin solving the mystery of how the plastic affected ocean life.

After weeks of preparation, the student scientists waved good-bye to their families from the deck of *New Horizon*. It shoved off from the pier in San Diego, California. They couldn't help wondering what they would find.

New Horizon is about as long as four school buses parked end to end. The five decks house a lab, a library, a laundry room, sleeping cabins, a kitchen, and more. The ship burns about 1,000 gallons (3,785 liters) of fuel a day and costs about $18,000 to $19,000 a day to run!

NEW HORIZON

GARBAGE, HERE WE COME!

ON AUGUST 2, 2009, Miriam, Chelsea, and Darcy sailed west as part of the Scripps Environmental Accumulation of Plastic Expedition (SEAPLEX). They headed toward an area of the Pacific Ocean full of millions—maybe billions—of plastic pieces. Scientists call the area the Great Pacific Garbage Patch. Racing boat captain Charles Moore discovered it in 1997. He found abandoned fishing nets, plastic bottles, bottle caps, toothbrushes, containers, boxes, and tiny pieces of plastic. The litter came from rivers and streams that flow into the ocean. It came from people visiting the beach or riding on ships who did not properly dispose

Supplies are loaded onto *New Horizon* with a crane. Everyone pitches in to load the ship.

of their plastic. Ocean currents carried it to the Garbage Patch.

Miriam and the other SEAPLEX scientists wanted to answer some important questions with their research. How much plastic was in the Garbage Patch? Were fish eating the plastic? If so, were they dying because of it? Were the chemicals used to make plastic poisoning the water? Did plastic affect the food chain? Were any animals and plants living on the floating plastic? And if so, were the plastic homes poisoning the animals? Team SEAPLEX hoped to find answers, but they also knew those answers would raise other questions.

TRASH TALK: THE PATH TO AN EXPERIMENT

Team SEAPLEX used the scientific method to find answers to their questions about the Garbage Patch. Their first step was observation. The trash detectives gathered samples of water and marine life. They studied these samples for patterns. They developed hypotheses, or predictions of what they would find. The scientists tested their hypotheses by designing experiments. The trash detectives' experiments answered some of their questions. Sometimes their experiments led to more questions!

In addition to Miriam, Chelsea, and Darcy, the team aboard *New Horizon* included four other students, their faculty adviser, eight volunteers, and twelve crew members. For the first day or two on the water, they struggled to find their sea legs. They tried to roll with the swells and not bump into walls while walking on deck. Some of them were seasick. They wore life jackets during safety drills. They learned how to get from their cabins to the galley (the kitchen). The team also tested their large nets by gathering samples of seawater and fish for observation. Everything—except the soda machine in the galley—worked perfectly.

When the scientists weren't working or sleeping, they read, lifted weights on the top deck, or climbed the stair stepper in the machine room. Space was tight on board *New Horizon*. The deck was full of bulky nets and wires. Chelsea and Miriam slept on bunk beds in a room so small only one of them could stand on the floor at a time.

Meanwhile, the crew piloted the ship on its weeklong journey out to the Garbage Patch.

Clockwise, from bottom left: The crew led safety drills onboard. They lifted weights to stay in shape while living on the ship. They also kept the team fed. The soda machine didn't give many options, but the ship made plenty of drinking water by filtering seawater.

They also fixed the broken soda machine and cooked meals. Once, a crew member even caught fresh fish for supper.

As *New Horizon* sailed farther from land, the trash detectives kept their eyes peeled. "We are hoping to see whales, birds, and maybe even some plastic," Chelsea wrote on the SEAPLEX blog. "It sounds sad to hope for trash. But if we don't find any, we can't address any of our questions. GARBAGE, HERE WE COME!"

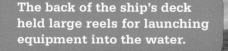

The back of the ship's deck held large reels for launching equipment into the water.

Top left: A crew member caught a dorado for supper. The trash detectives dissected the fish before eating it!

Bottom left: Trash detectives searched for birds and plastic on the bridge deck next to *New Horizon*'s pilothouse.

Below: A black-footed albatross was seen on Day 7 off the back of *New Horizon*.

BRAVING THE GYRE

WITHIN A DAY OF LEAVING SAN DIEGO, blue sky merged with blue water all around. Fish fed. Birds soared. Land was only a memory.

Miriam and her team sailed toward the North Pacific Central Gyre, where the Great Pacific Garbage Patch is located. The gyre is an area of the ocean three times bigger than the United States, not including Alaska and Hawaii. Four ocean currents form the boundaries of the gyre: the North Pacific Current, the California Current, the North Equatorial Current, and the Kuroshio Current. Wind patterns cause these currents to rotate in a clockwise direction. They travel from south of Alaska down the western coast of North America, to the equator, and toward Japan. The Hawaiian Islands sit inside the gyre. Compared to the currents surrounding it, the water inside the gyre is relatively calm.

GREAT PACIFIC
GARBAGE PATCH
(North Pacific Central Gyre)

NORTH PACIFIC

KUROSHIO

CALIFORNIA

NORTH EQUATORIAL

Hawaiian Islands

■ Newport,
Oregon

■ San Diego, California

ASIA

NORTH AMERICA

SOUTH AMERICA

AUSTRALIA

warm
current

cold
current

route of
the *New
Horizon*

OCEAN SCIENCE: SQUID ALERT!

One day, Miriam spotted a huge rotting squid floating in the water. "I got to yell, 'Captain! Follow that squid!'" she recalled. The trash detectives hauled the body aboard. "I stuck my hand in its eye," Chelsea said, "and pulled out an eyeball the size of a tennis ball!" Miriam saved samples of the squid before throwing the smelly beast back into the ocean. "It's unlikely that its death was related to plastic," Miriam said. "Most plastic is on the surface, and squid live deep." But some things are too cool for a scientist to pass up.

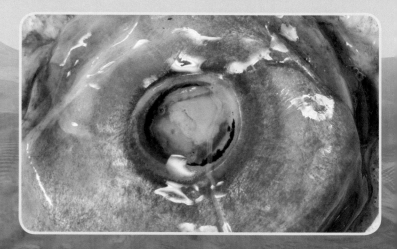

The trash detectives thought that the squid might have been about 16 to 19 feet (5 to 6 meters) long. They preserved the eye *(above)* and the beak *(bottom right)* for later study. Squid use their sharp beaks to rip apart prey.

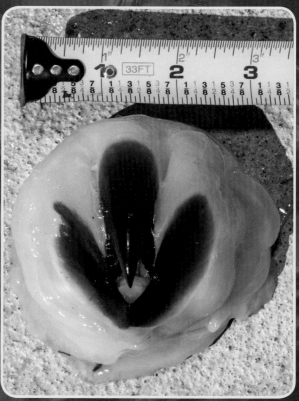

Miriam called the gyre a liquid desert. On the surface, it appears almost lifeless. Upon closer inspection, several kinds of animals call it home. Tiny creatures in the gyre hitch rides on other animals or floating debris. Scientists call these creatures the rafting community. Small crabs hide in the leathery folds between a sea turtle's tail and shell. Barnacles drift on a feather or a dead bird. Fish lay eggs on a floating log.

The plastic in the gyre—several tons of it—also floats near the surface. Wind, tides, and smaller ocean currents carry debris from shore. Larger currents catch the plastic and carry it to the gyre. The plastic rarely escapes because of the currents that circle the gyre.

Many people picture the Garbage Patch as an enormous floating island. The reality is different. It doesn't look like a mass of garbage from the air. It's hardly visible from the deck of a ship. Many of the plastic pieces started out as water bottles, milk jugs, pool toys, action figures, Legos, or toothbrushes. Most have broken down into pieces no bigger than a kernel of unpopped popcorn.

Every day SEAPLEX trash detectives looked over the side of the ship for plastic pieces. They counted the number they saw.

After five days at sea, pieces of plastic began to float by the ship. Two scientists on the top deck, about 30 feet (10 m) above the water, counted one hundred pieces during the day shift. The closer the trash detectives sailed to the gyre, the more plastic they saw.

MIRIAM'S HITCHHIKERS

MIRIAM LOVED POKING AROUND TIDE POOLS AS A KID. In ninth grade, she discovered that she could have a career as an ocean scientist. "I had no idea that people could learn about weird, slimy marine creatures for a living. I've been hooked ever since!" she said.

On board *New Horizon*, Miriam studied how plastic affects the rafting community— the tiny organisms that hitch rides on plastic pieces. Did fish lay eggs on plastic? Did barnacles live on floating plastic? Did organisms travel to parts of the ocean where they did not belong? Miriam hoped the samples she gathered would provide answers. The ocean forms a web of interconnected communities. If the presence of plastic changed one community, it could affect the whole ecosystem.

On Day 7 of the SEAPLEX voyage, *New*

Horizon arrived at the gyre. Miriam could finally begin observing the hitchhikers scooped up in the net tows. For safety reasons, only one piece of equipment could be in the water at a time. So when one net came in, another one went out. The scientists on duty examined each incoming net for fish, tiny organisms called plankton, and pieces of plastic.

Miriam was supposed to work the night shift, from 8:00 p.m. to 8:00 a.m., and sleep during the day. In reality, she worked many nights and days. By Day 8, Miriam and her team hauled plastic pieces aboard in every net tow. For a closer view, some of the team climbed aboard an inflatable boat. Miriam described it as "a flying fish-eyed view of the gyre." The glassy water mirrored the sky's brilliant blue. The water was so clear that sunlight reached 450 feet (137 m) below the surface. Plastic pieces large and small dotted the surface.

Miriam floated a quadrat on the

Above: A single piece of blue plastic is home to several flying fish eggs.

Below: Some of the SEAPLEX team haul a ghost net aboard the inflatable boat with a dip net.

water. This square of plastic pipe is roughly 3 by 3 feet (1 by 1 m). The quadrat helped the scientists estimate the amount of plastic at the surface. They counted the pieces of plastic floating inside one square. Some quadrats had no plastic inside the square. Others had up to eleven pieces. The trash detectives calculated the average number of pieces per quadrat. They multiplied that by the 7 to 9 million square miles (18 to 23 million sq. km) of gyre. That's a lot of plastic 1,000 miles (1,609 km) or more from land!

The detectives scooped plastic into handheld dip nets. Some pieces were no bigger than a grain of rice. Others were larger, such as water bottles, parts of old buckets, and buoys. Barnacles, crabs, fish eggs, and anemones coated the undersides of the plastic. They feed on phytoplankton and zooplankton—the smallest plant and animal organisms in the ocean.

Top: Miriam counts the number of plastic pieces in the quadrat.

Bottom: This ocean buoy was found with hundreds of gooseneck barnacles growing on it.

OCEAN SCIENCE: SCIENCE TOYS

SEAPLEX scientists used several types of nets to find out what was in the water at different depths.

MANTA NETS have two wings like a manta ray. The wings help the net float at the surface. The net's fine mesh collects small bits of plastic and zooplankton.

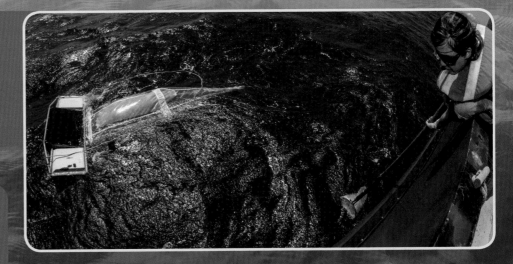

BONGO NETS look like a pair of bongo drums attached to a metal frame. *New Horizon* tows the nets about 656 feet (200 m) below the surface. Like the manta nets, the fine mesh captures zooplankton and plastic in deeper water.

OOZEKI TRAWLS sample water between 1,300 and 6,600 feet (396 and 2,011 m) deep. These nets are 6 feet (1.8 m) wide at the mouth and about 20 feet (6.1 m) long. They collect small fish and large crustaceans (sea creatures with a hard shell), such as krill.

Back in *New Horizon*'s lab, Miriam and her team rinsed, sorted, saved, and recorded every sample collected. Then they stored the samples in jars and test tubes, which were placed in coolers or plastic bins for later study.

"It is impossible to look at each piece carefully at sea," Miriam said. Large manta nets, bongo nets, and Oozeki trawls brought more plastic debris aboard every hour. But Miriam required two to four hours to study the organisms on each piece. She also preferred to have two feet on dry land before she peered through a microscope. The tiny creatures sloshed back and forth in their containers as the ship rose and fell. "Nothing gets your seasickness going like microscope work on the ocean," she said.

Some trash detectives braved the sloshing to inspect small animals called bryozoans and hydroids. Bryozoans look like visitors from another planet with coral-like shells. Hydroids, relatives of jellies, live on the surface and look like plants. These two kinds of creatures floated on plastic rafts and fed on microscopic organisms in the water. Miriam realized the millions of pieces of plastic pollution were like empty homes tempting the rafting community to move in.

As a result, the desertlike gyre seemed to have become a major metropolis of rafters. What would all this new life mean for the gyre?

When Miriam returned to San Diego, she reviewed the data she'd collected. Then she designed an experiment. Miriam tested how

Miriam holds a petri dish of confetti-sized plastic pieces.

Top: This is one of the hundreds of sample jars collected on the SEAPLEX voyage. It contains bits of colored plastic, dark blue *Velella velella* jellies, and beige plankton.

Bottom left: Mussels, crabs, and sea anemones live on a piece of discarded rope.

Bottom right: This sample shows *Halobates*, insects that can live on the surface of the ocean, and tiny plastic pieces. Miriam wondered how the floating ocean plastic might affect these insects.

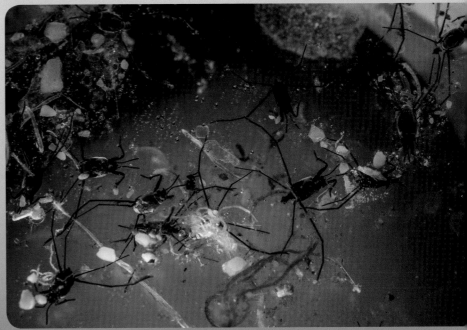

the amount of plastic in the water affected one rafter, an ocean insect called *Halobates*. Her hypothesis predicted that more plastic would allow *Halobates* to lay more eggs. She found that the amount of plastic in a given area of the ocean was already about one hundred times greater than it was in the 1970s. She also found that *Halobates* took advantage of the floating plastic to lay more eggs than in the 1970s. *Halobates* feed on zooplankton.

Miriam wondered about other creatures that ate zooplankton. If many more *Halobates* hatched—and ate zooplankton—than in previous years, would they cause others to go hungry?

All the hydroids, bryozoans, and barnacles that float into the Garbage Patch on plastic eat zooplankton too. Miriam wondered if these hitchhikers could change the food chain—the who-eats-whom—in the gyre. Zooplankton are

OCEAN SCIENCE: WHO EATS WHAT?

To see the balance of life and death in the North Pacific Central Gyre, look no further than the food chain. Plants called phytoplankton grow using the sun's energy and nutrients from the water. Microscopic animals called zooplankton eat the phytoplankton. Tiny creatures such as copepods filter zooplankton from the water as food. Bigger fish eat the copepods. When an ocean creature dies, bacteria decompose its body. Decomposition releases nutrients back to the ocean to feed the phytoplankton.

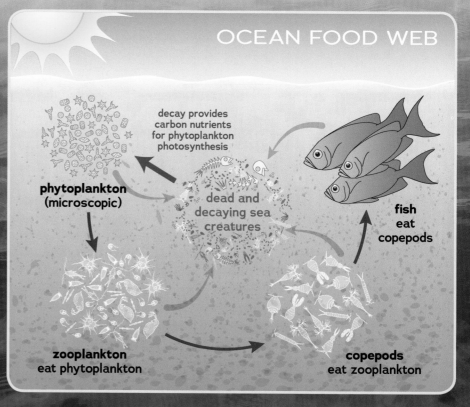

OCEAN FOOD WEB

decay provides carbon nutrients for phytoplankton photosynthesis

phytoplankton (microscopic)

dead and decaying sea creatures

fish eat copepods

zooplankton eat phytoplankton

copepods eat zooplankton

The ship's lab was about one-third the size of a basketball court. But it was jammed with science equipment. In addition, the scientists packed cameras, journals, handheld dip nets, microscope slides, collection bottles, computers, and plenty of sunscreen. They tied down their equipment to keep it from rolling around at sea.

a critical link in the food chain. But they are not naturally plentiful in the gyre. What would happen if there were not enough to go around? Would the fish that eat these small creatures starve? What would happen to large fish that eat small fish? Would fish leave the gyre to find food?

Finding these answers provides a key to understanding the effects of the ocean plastic. "We have a long way to go," Miriam said.

DARCY FOLLOWS PHYTOPLANKTON

WHEN SEAPLEX TRASH DETECTIVE DARCY TANIGUCHI WAS A KID, she visited Monterey Bay Aquarium in Monterey, California. The ocean fascinated her. She loved studying sea life. "Wouldn't it be cool if that were your job?" she asked herself.

Darcy was living her dream as a graduate student on SEAPLEX. She gathered phytoplankton, tiny one-celled plants, along *New Horizon*'s path to the North Pacific Central Gyre. She wanted to compare the types and numbers of phytoplankton near the shore with those found on or near plastic in the gyre. Her goal was to find out how the plastic affected these organisms.

The ocean contains many kinds of phytoplankton. "They come in all shapes and sizes," Darcy said. "Some are little round

Left: **SEAPLEX trash detective Darcy Taniguchi works at the seawater filtration system. She filters out plastic and marine life to study the carbon in the water. The amount of carbon helps her measure the number of phytoplankton living in the gyre.**

Below: **These bits of plastic were caught in the filter.**

circles, some are like rocket ships, some are like cylinders." Some phytoplankton swim to move through the water, while others drift. All perform photosynthesis. They make their own food energy from carbon dioxide and sunlight, just as plants on land do. Some also eat to get energy. "And it's all contained within one single cell," Darcy marveled, "compared to humans that are made of trillions of cells."

We cannot see most phytoplankton with the naked eye. They can be as small as 1 micrometer (0.001 millimeter, or 0.00004 inches) or as large as half a centimeter (0.2 inches). But in the water, they're everywhere. "Every

time we swim, we swallow tons of these guys," Darcy said. One milliliter of river, lake, or ocean water (less than a quarter teaspoon) contains between ten thousand and one hundred thousand phytoplankton!

Like all plants, phytoplankton give off oxygen. They release it as a product of photosynthesis. In fact, the ocean contains so many phytoplankton that they produce half to two-thirds of all of Earth's oxygen. That means they make the oxygen for nearly two of every three breaths we take! "They are the grass of the ocean," Darcy said. "Life could not exist as we know it without them."

Providing that much oxygen is an important job. But phytoplankton do even more. They consume carbon dioxide during photosynthesis. This reduces the amount of carbon in our environment. Scientists believe extra carbon in the air is the main cause of global warming (rising average temperatures on Earth). So by taking carbon dioxide out of the air, phytoplankton may help fight the warming trend.

In addition, phytoplankton are the first link in the ocean food chain. Every ocean creature, no matter how large or small, depends on these tiny plants.

If plastic harms the phytoplankton population, Earth's oxygen supply could suffer. Eventually every creature in the sea could go hungry. We could go hungry too. Seafood feeds

OCEAN SCIENCE:
OCEAN OXYGEN, A PERFECT BALANCE

To grow and survive, phytoplankton need sunlight and nutrients. Chlorophyll inside the phytoplankton absorbs the sun's energy. Then phytoplankton absorb carbon nutrients that dead creatures have released into the water. The combination of carbon, energy, and seawater makes sugar to feed the phytoplankton. Oxygen is released as a waste product. And humans need oxygen to breathe. It's a perfectly balanced system.

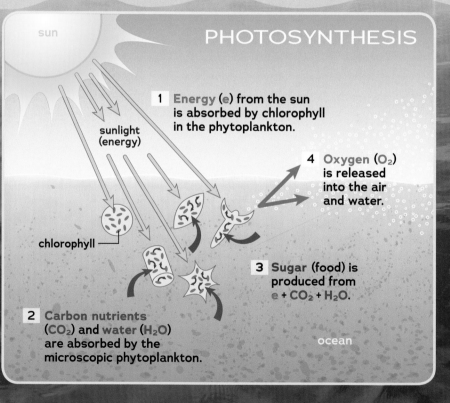

PHOTOSYNTHESIS

sun

1 Energy (e) from the sun is absorbed by chlorophyll in the phytoplankton.

sunlight (energy)

chlorophyll

4 Oxygen (O_2) is released into the air and water.

3 Sugar (food) is produced from $e + CO_2 + H_2O$.

2 Carbon nutrients (CO_2) and water (H_2O) are absorbed by the microscopic phytoplankton.

ocean

about 3 billion people worldwide. And nearly one-tenth of the world's population relies on the fishing industry for income. For them, no fish means no work.

Darcy and other scientists around the world are worried about the changing number of phytoplankton in the ocean. Some studies show a sharp decrease since the 1940s. But no one knows why. Scientists need to learn more about phytoplankton growth and their habits.

Phytoplankton sometimes die from a virus, kind of like a dangerous case of the flu. And sometimes phytoplankton die off because they can't develop normally. Scientists call this programmed cell death. Suppose plastic in the water changed the way phytoplankton develop. Would more die than usual? Would they be more likely to catch viruses? Darcy hoped to solve these mysteries by studying the phytoplankton in different areas of the ocean.

Before the voyage, Darcy didn't know if phytoplankton were eating the ocean plastic. But once she observed the gyre herself, she predicted that they were not. Even though most of the plastic was no bigger than a pencil

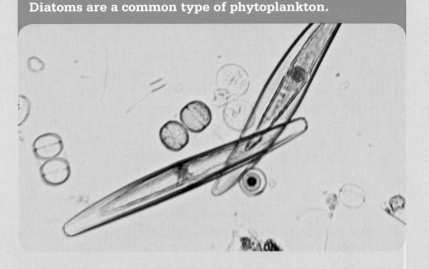

Diatoms are a common type of phytoplankton.

eraser, it was still too large for microscopic phytoplankton to eat.

Darcy did know before the voyage that the farther from shore she sailed, the deeper phytoplankton lived. "Light penetrates further," she said. So phytoplankton in the gyre capture sunlight at greater depths than those near the shore. But she had wondered if there was enough plastic to block the sunlight in the deep ocean. Once she saw the gyre for herself, Darcy predicted there was not. Although millions of plastic pieces float in the gyre, they were not big enough to shade large areas. Phytoplankton could still make food

TRASH TALK: PERMANENT PLASTIC

Consider the dead squid that the SEAPLEX team found on its cruise. The squid floats on the water. It decomposes in the bright sunlight. It stinks, but fish feed on its dead tissue. The rotting squid releases carbon into the water, which feeds phytoplankton. It continues biodegrading—breaking down—into the basic elements of life. It is no longer a squid.

Consider a plastic water bottle. It is not made of biological substances that feed fish or help phytoplankton perform photosynthesis. The water bottle photodegrades. Over time, sunlight and wave motion break the plastic into smaller and smaller pieces. But the pieces are still plastic—and will be for perhaps thousands of years.

through photosynthesis.

On board *New Horizon*, Darcy took measurements. She set up the CTD (conductivity, temperature, depth) Rosette, an instrument that collects water at different depths. The CTD measured the glow of chlorophyll inside phytoplankton. Darcy used these measurements to estimate the number of phytoplankton in the gyre.

After the SEAPLEX voyage, Darcy's research took a new turn. Her adviser suggested she study another part of the ocean to determine how quickly phytoplankton grow and die. She never experimented with her data from the gyre on the numbers and sizes of phytoplankton. Many of Darcy's questions went unanswered. Her experience is common in research. New questions and hypotheses pop up that send scientists in new directions.

However, the connection between plastic and phytoplankton remains an important part of the plastic mystery for scientists. "The next time you cup seawater in your hands," Darcy said, "realize that you hold within your grasp organisms which are crucial for sustaining life."

Darcy *(top and below, right)* and Meg Rippy *(below, left)* prepare the CTD Rosette for launch. The attached bottles collect water samples at different depths. Sensors measure temperature, depth, and the amount of salt in the water. Some CTDs also measure the amount of oxygen and light in the water. Timbo Stillinger and Chelsea *(far left)* use ropes to ease the CTD into the water.

CHELSEA'S PLASTIC PUZZLE

CHELSEA MARINA ROCHMAN'S PARENTS MAY HAVE THOUGHT SHE WAS BORN TO STUDY THE SEA. Her middle name means "seaside" in Spanish and Italian. In high school, she ditched school for Earth Day to help with beach cleanups. Her interest in the ocean continued to grow, and she decided to become a marine scientist.

Chelsea's specialty is the chemistry of plastic. She was concerned about the chemicals in the plastic bits floating in the ocean. Most plastics begin with petroleum (oil). Added chemicals help shape plastics for specific purposes. For instance, plastic casings around computers, televisions, and electrical wires are coated with chemicals that reduce the risk of fire. Different chemicals soften the plastic in plastic wrap and squeeze toys.

However, the added chemicals don't always stay in plastic. SEAPLEX scientists already knew that chemicals seep out of plastic debris as it floats in the sunlit ocean. Chelsea hoped to answer some questions about the chemicals possibly seeping from plastic in the gyre. Did chemicals from the plastic harm marine life? Did the plastic also carry other pollutants? If so, were those pollutants harming other areas of the ocean? Did the plastic bits soak up chemicals released into the ocean by other plastics?

OCEAN SCIENCE: MUNCHING MICROBES

Scientists think plastic might float in the ocean for thousands of years before it fully breaks down. In 2008, a Canadian teenager designed an experiment to try to decompose plastic more quickly on land. He mixed bits of plastic with water, yeast, and landfill dirt (loaded with bacteria). He let the mixture stew. The plastic disappeared in three months, thanks to bacteria eating the plastic. No one knows if we would see the same results in the ocean. If plastic in the gyre could disappear in months instead of years, Chelsea wonders at what cost to the ocean bacteria. Would they absorb the poisonous plastic chemicals like fish?

Irish scientists are taking the teen's research one step further. They cooked plastic water bottles and fed them to plastic-munching microbes. The microbes digest the plastic and turn it into a new kind of biodegradable plastic that breaks down more quickly. These microbes could help plastic trash decompose in landfills and in the ocean.

However, Chelsea worries that people might think biodegradable plastic solves the problem. "It's like slapping a Band-Aid on the problem and saying it's okay if the plastic ends up as litter because it's biodegradable."

Chelsea and Pete Davison rinse the oozeki trawl *(left)*. Jellies, lanternfish, vampire squid, hatchet fish, and other organisms in the net are funneled to the cod end. Then Pete empties the cod end for the lab *(right)*.

Many chemicals added to plastic are poisonous to mice. At high concentrations, they can even harm humans. Some of these chemicals disrupt cell growth, cell reproduction, and communication between cells. Others may cause tumors. So Chelsea designed an experiment to find out if marine life in the gyre absorbed chemicals from the plastic.

On board *New Horizon*, Chelsea set up

A chain of salps floats in the ocean.

net tows and gathered samples with her fellow trash detectives on the day shift. They preserved thousands of jellylike salps that floated on the surface. (Chelsea thought they looked like "someone hocked a loogie.")

Chelsea's hypothesis predicted she'd see evidence of plastic chemicals in the salps. And she did! What's more, she discovered that the salps from the areas with the most plastic had the highest concentration of chemicals.

These results sent Chelsea to the next question. Did plastics in the ocean absorb chemicals already polluting the water? And if so, would fish absorb those pollutants as well?

Chelsea predicted that the answer to both questions would be *yes*. To find out, she designed a new experiment when she returned home. She fed three groups of fish different diets. Group A ate regular fish food. Group B ate ground-up plastic that had never

TRASH TALK: NURDLES AND TRIANGLES

Plastic comes from oil made into small pellets called nurdles. Different kinds of nurdles yield different kinds of plastic, such as water bottles, margarine tubs, and paint buckets. Look for the small triangle on plastic items at home. The number inside the triangle indicates the type of nurdle used. These numbers help us figure out how to recycle the plastic.

In the ocean, different plastics absorb different amounts of chemicals from the water. The worst offenders are plastics with recycling codes of two, four, and five. We use these plastics in yogurt containers, milk jugs, cereal box liners, squeeze bottles, bread bags, bottle caps, and straws. "They are manufactured in greater quantities," Chelsea says. "They also absorb the most contaminants." But none of the numbers mean it's okay to throw the plastic in the ocean.

Top: Chelsea and Miriam record information on the data sheet about every net tow or CTD collection. The sheet keeps track of when each device enters and leaves the water, the wind speed, and whether the sea was calm or rough.

Bottom: The trash detectives worked long hours on *New Horizon*. The bean bag chair was a popular place to read (or catch a nap)!

been in the ocean. Group C ate ground-up plastic that was first soaked in seawater polluted with chemicals. As expected, Chelsea found higher concentrations of chemicals in the tissues of both groups that ate the plastic. The chemical levels were highest in the tissues of Group C fish, which ate the plastic soaked in seawater. The fish absorbed chemicals from the plastic *and* the toxins the plastic had absorbed. "The fish poop out the plastic, but the chemicals stay in their muscles and fat," Chelsea said.

Chelsea also hypothesized that the plastic she fed her fish filled their stomachs, so they weren't hungry for real food. The plastic was like junk food. It did not supply nutrients for the fish to live. Chelsea concluded that a double dose of plastic and poisonous chemicals means double the threat for fish in the gyre.

Chelsea's experiments show that sea life in the gyre might be in serious danger because of the Garbage Patch. The open ocean is no

Chelsea and Doug, another trash detective, examine a dip net.

longer a wild place untouched by humans. At 1,000 miles (1,600 km) from land, SEAPLEX scientists saw evidence of human pollution in almost every net tow. Poisonous chemicals in plastic contaminate the water. And organisms such as salps soak up the toxins as they drift.

CHARTING THE ANSWERS

THE SEAPLEX TRASH DETECTIVES found plastic in 130 of their 132 net tows over 1,700 miles (2,736 km) of open ocean. That's the same distance as between New York City and Denver, Colorado. "To see plastic debris in the middle of this large stretch of ocean, far from land," Chelsea said, "offers a wake-up call for the way we leave our footprint even on remote places of the Earth."

The SEAPLEX team had even more questions about ocean plastic after their cruise. For instance, how long had the plastic been in the gyre? The scientists couldn't tell from their samples. Miriam began an experiment to age plastic on the roof of her lab in San Diego. She put plastic and seawater in several containers. Some containers were in the sun. Some were in the dark. With the results, she hoped to be able to estimate the age of ocean plastic.

Darcy wondered if plastic determined how fast phytoplankton are eaten. Perhaps animals that eat phytoplankton found plastic to be tastier. Would they choose plastic junk food over the phytoplankton?

Chelsea found that fish receive a double

These tiny fish and plastic pieces were captured inside a 3:00 a.m. manta net tow.

dose of plastic poison from the water and the plastic they eat. So how much plastic ends up in the fish people eat? Back in San Diego,

⬦OCEAN SCIENCE: NATURE'S LIGHT SHOW

Nighttime in the gyre is very dark. *New Horizon* sailed at night using advanced navigation equipment. Occasionally, the ship's wake excited bacteria, single-celled algae, or animals to light up the water. The light came from a chemical reaction inside the organisms called bioluminescence. Many sea creatures use bioluminescence to scare or confuse predators. They also use their lights to confuse prey or spotlight it in the deep, dark ocean.

On Day 20 of the voyage, one of Miriam's team members woke her up to see something at 3 a.m. "I staggered outside in my stripy pajamas," Miriam said. "Fiery bioluminescence erupted from our wake and from each whitecap all the way to the horizon. . . . The stars mirrored the glowing sea." Miriam ran to wake Chelsea. "It was the most beautiful thing I've ever seen, hands down," Chelsea says.

California, two SEAPLEX scientists conducted an experiment dissecting fish samples from the voyage. They found plastic in the stomachs of nearly one out of every ten fish. They also estimated that fish in the middle depths of the North Pacific eat about 12,000 to 24,000 tons (10,884 to 21,768 metric tons) of plastic per year. This estimate could be low. The trash detectives did not measure plastic that the fish vomit or poop. They also did not measure the number of fish that died from plastic poisoning.

These results showed that plastic has entered the food chain in the gyre. If a shark at the top of the food chain ate one hundred fish, nine would contain plastic.

A number of groups are helping scientists learn more about ocean plastic. The Scripps Institute of Oceanography sponsored the SEAPLEX graduate students. Project Kaisei also helped fund SEAPLEX. This group

organizes expeditions to the North Pacific Central Gyre to study ocean plastic and ways to clean it up. In 2009, Kaisei teamed up with tech company Ojingo Labs. They shared their expeditions with the world in real time through video blogging and a voyage tracker created with Google Earth. People could pinpoint where plastic was collected. They could get a firsthand look at the Garbage Patch. Project Kaisei was named a Google Earth Hero for its work.

The Algalita Marine Research Institute

With Project Kaisei's voyage tracker, people could watch a video from the expedition and see exactly where in the ocean it had been shot.

also studies the plastic problem in the North Pacific. The organization was founded by Captain Charles Moore, who discovered the Great Pacific Garbage Patch. The group shares its findings with lawmakers, educators, and people like us.

The National Oceanic and Atmospheric Administration (NOAA) studies the health of Earth's air and water. As part of its work, this government agency sponsors research on marine debris. It also prepares educational materials for schools and meets with other groups to discuss solutions to the worldwide plastic problem.

Some groups are exploring ocean plastic in other areas too. Plastic debris floats in each of five large gyres around the globe. Sea Education Association (SEA), of Woods Hole, Massachusetts, has sailed to both the North Atlantic Gyre and the North Pacific Central Gyre. SEA scientists study the marine life and plastic pieces gathered in net tows at each gyre.

In one study, SEA scientists examined bacteria living on plastic. They counted seven

TRASH TALK: MAKING A DIFFERENCE

The Ocean Conservancy works to keep the ocean healthy, so we stay healthy. Every year, this organization sponsors a worldwide beach cleanup day *(below)*. In 2012, nearly 562,000 volunteers picked up trash along 17,719 miles (28,516 km) of coastline. They collected more than 10 million pounds (4.6 million kilograms) of trash (the weight of 113 humpback whales or 725 male African elephants). Cigarettes, food wrappers, and plastic drink bottles topped the list of items found. The group also rescued fish, mammals, reptiles, and birds tangled in traps, nets, and plastic fishing line.

thousand different kinds of bacteria on *one* piece half the size of your pinkie nail! Bacteria formed the building blocks of a mini-ecosystem on each tiny scrap. They gave off carbon, which attracted one-celled organisms that performed photosynthesis. Other microscopic creatures called grazers ate the one-celled organisms. Then tiny predators captured the grazers and sucked them dry. The bacteria, one-celled organisms, grazers, and predators were like the Whos of *Horton Hears a Who!*, by Dr. Seuss, building an entire city on a speck of dust. The SEA scientists had discovered a marine Whoville on each bit of plastic. But is the plastic harming the life it supports? And would the Whovilles exist in the gyre without plastic?

Unfortunately, scientists cannot solve the plastic problem through research alone. They

Trash litters this beach in Indonesia. Unfortunately, many beaches around the world have the same problem.

need help from kids and adults everywhere. Plastic is a permanent material used in disposable products. And it is accumulating in all five major gyres around the globe. So what can we do about it?

First, "people need to change their habits," Chelsea said. "No more single-use convenience plastic. We don't need it." The following changes are a good place to start:

Carry a washable storage container to restaurants for leftovers instead of requesting a take-home box.

Bring reusable bags to the grocery store instead of taking new plastic (or paper) bags each time. For fruits and vegetables, use recycled paper bags instead of plastic bags.

Wash and reuse plastic forks, spoons, and knives instead of throwing them out after one use. Better yet, buy compostable utensils or bring your own!

Carry a stainless steel bottle for water instead of buying plastic bottles. For groups or parties, provide a large pitcher of water with reusable cups rather than individual water bottles.

Use washable mugs for coffee instead of cups made from plastic that is not recyclable.

Don't buy products that come with a lot of plastic packaging. Instead, buy products from companies that use recycled plastic or glass. For example, the Method soap company gathers plastic washed ashore in Hawaii. The company recycles the plastic to make new soap bottles for its products.

Write to companies and encourage them to use recycled packaging—and less packaging overall.

Brainstorm a list of other ways to help, and share it with your family and your classmates.

In addition to changing personal habits, become an ocean educator. Give the ocean a voice by helping others become aware of plastic pollution. Try some of these ideas:

Collect empty soda cans, plastic bottles, and glass bottles. Take them to the recycling center. How much money can you earn? Consider making this a schoolwide project.

Participate in a beach cleanup day at a nearby ocean, lake, or river.

Create a plastic-free day (or week) at school—no disposable plastic bottles, utensils, or bags allowed!

Carry the plastic you use around for a week to raise awareness of how much you use during that time.

Most important, talk to family and friends about the plastic in our oceans. Be the person who urges everyone to recycle.

The ocean provides the air we breathe, the food we eat, a place to play, and a place to admire nature. Yet plastic floats in ocean waters around the world. "The ocean is the cradle of life on Earth," Miriam said. Plastic pollution may threaten our greatest resource.

SEAPLEX research shows that the floating plastic is already a problem. Scientists are just beginning to understand how many ways it may be affecting Earth's vast ocean. Taking action right away may keep the Great Pacific Garbage Patch from growing much larger and having an even greater effect on the ocean and Earth. "People want to know that there are wildernesses out there somewhere," Miriam said. "If even the open sea is no longer a wilderness, what is?"

"Perhaps," Miriam said, "missions like SEAPLEX will become obsolete, and ocean science will be done for the sheer joy of discovery instead of the necessity of understanding what our species has wrought."

SOURCE NOTES

10 Chelsea Rochman, "SEAPLEX Day 1," *SEAPLEX* (blog), August, 2, 2009, http://seaplexscience.com /2009/08/02/seaplex-day-1/.

14 Miriam Goldstein, "SEAPLEX Day 1," *SEAPLEX* (blog), August 6, 2009, http://seaplexscience.com/2009 /08/06/seaplex-day-5-part-2/.

14 Rochman, comments to the author about the manuscript text, January 9, 2013.

14 Goldstein, e-mail to the author, May 5, 2012.

16 Goldstein, "Interview with Miriam Goldstein—in Which We Discuss Plastic Debris, Cool Sea Creatures, Science Usability and More," My Aquarium Club, Ruth's Blog, March 9, 2011, at http://www .myaquariumclub.com/interview-with-miriam -goldstein-in-which-we-discuss-plastic-debris-cool -sea-creatures-science-usability-and-more-642.html.

17 Goldstein, "SEAPLEX Day 14," *SEAPLEX* (blog), August 15, 2009, http://seaplexscience.com/ 2009/08/15/seaplex-day-14/.

18 Jesse Dubler, "SEAPLEX Day 14," *SEAPLEX* (blog), August 18, 2009, http://seaplexscience.com/ 2009/08/18/367/.

20 Goldstein, interview with the author, September 5, 2012.

20 Ibid.

20 Ibid.

24 Darcy Taniguchi, interview with the author, November 5, 2012.

24–25 Ibid.

25 Ibid.

25 Ibid.

26 Ibid.

27 Ibid.

28 Taniguchi, "SEAPLEX Day 16," *SEAPLEX* (blog), August 17, 2009, http://seaplexscience.com/2009/08/17/seaplex -day-16/.

31 Rochman, interview with the author, October 28, 2009.

33 Ibid.

34 Rochman, interview with the author, October 30, 2012.

35 Ibid.

36 Rochman, "SEAPLEX Day 8 Part 2," *SEAPLEX* (blog), August 9, 2009, http://seaplexscience.com/2009/08/09 /seaplex-day-8-part-2/.

37 Goldstein, "SEAPLEX Day 20 Part 3: The Last Blog from Sea," *SEAPLEX* (blog), August 21, 2009, http:// seaplexscience.com/2009/08/21/seaplex-day-20-part-3 -the-last-blog-from-sea/.

37 Rochman, comments about the manuscript text.

41 Rochman, interview with the author, October 28, 2009.

42 Goldstein, "SEAPLEX Day 20 Part 3."

42 Goldstein, "SEAPLEX Day 19," SEAPLEX (blog), August 20, 2009, http://seaplexscience.com/2009/08/20/seaplex -day-19/.

43 Goldstein, "SEAPLEX Day 20 Part 3."

GLOSSARY

anemones: colorful sea animals that look like flowers and paralyze their prey with stinging tentacles

barnacles: sea creatures with a hard shell that attach themselves to floating ocean debris, on the bottoms of boats, and to piers

bryozoans: sea creatures that form shells resembling coral

carbon dioxide: a gas exhaled by humans and most other living organisms. Phytoplankton and other plants use carbon dioxide in photosynthesis.

chlorophyll: a green pigment found in all land and marine plants. It absorbs the sun's energy for photosynthesis.

contaminants: substances that pollute the ocean and Earth

copepods: tiny sea creatures found throughout the ocean that feed larger marine life

current: a stream of water that flows in one direction

ecosystem: a group of living things that interact in their environment

global warming: the warming of Earth's atmosphere and oceans due to an increase in greenhouse gases such as carbon dioxide

Halobates: a marine insect related to a water strider that looks like a spider with long legs

microbes: one-celled microscopic organisms

microscope: a scientific instrument used to study tiny objects

organism: a living creature that carries on the functions of life and is dependent on its environment

phytoplankton: microscopic one-celled marine plants. They create half to two-thirds of Earth's oxygen through photosynthesis.

plankton: a group of tiny marine animals or plants

predator: an animal that lives by killing and eating other animals

salps: barrel-shaped creatures that pump seawater through their bodies to strain out the phytoplankton they eat

zooplankton: tiny marine animals that feed on other plankton

FURTHER READING

BOOKS

Burns, Loree Griffin. *Tracking Trash: Flotsam, Jetsam and the Science of Ocean Motion*. New York: Houghton Mifflin, 2007. Follow one ocean detective as he investigates how sneakers and more end up in the ocean and where currents take them.

Gray, Susan Heinrichs. *Oceanography: The Study of Oceans*. New York: Scholastic, 2012. Get the basics on how scientists study the ocean.

Johnson, Rebecca L. *A Journey into the Ocean*. Minneapolis: Lerner Publications, 2004. Explore the ocean biome, the community of living things that thrives there.

Wilcox, Charlotte. *Earth-Friendly Waste Management*. Minneapolis: Lerner Publications Company, 2009. Find out Earth-friendly ways to deal with trash and keep it out of the ocean—and what you can do to help.

WEBSITES

Annie Crawley—YouTube
http://www.youtube.com/playlist?list=PL93615C0CBE9D7ACA
Check out lots of videos of the SEAPLEX team in action on the ocean from the photographer aboard *New Horizon*.

The Five Gyres Institute
http://5gyres.org/#
Explore the plastic problem more and find ways to help.

"Inside the Plastic Vortex"
http://www.youtube.com/watch?v=VT4GUhWMjog
Watch SEAPLEX scientists in action aboard *New Horizon*.

The Majestic Plastic Bag—a Mockumentary
http://www.youtube.com/watch?v=GLgh9h2ePYw&feature=player_embedded
This "mock"umentary chronicles the migration of the plastic bag toward the North Pacific Central Gyre.

National Ocean and Atmospheric Administration's Marine Debris Program
http://marinedebris.noaa.gov/
This program supports national and international efforts to research, prevent, and reduce the impacts of marine debris.

"Plastics at SEA, North Pacific Expedition"
http://www.sea.edu/plastics
Daily log entries, images, and videos are available at this site.

Project Kaisei
http://www.projectkaisei.org
View videos and photos of Kaisei's expeditions.

LERNER
e
SOURCE

Expand learning beyond the printed book. Download free, complementary educational resources for this book from our website, www.lernerresource.com.

INDEX

ABOUT THE AUTHOR

PATRICIA NEWMAN is the author of several books for children,

photograph by Kendall Newman

including *Jingle the Brass*, a Junior Library Guild Selection and a Smithsonian-recommended book, and *Nugget on the Flight Deck*, a California Reading Association Eureka! Silver Honor Book for Nonfiction. Patricia enjoys doing research and learning new things while working on her nonfiction books. In her spare time, she travels, reads, river rafts, and bakes yummy desserts. Visit her at www.patriciamnewman.com.

ABOUT THE PHOTOGRAPHER

photograph by Terry Keffler

ANNIE CRAWLEY graduated with a journalism degree from the University of Illinois. After learning to scuba dive and sail, she wanted to change the way the next generation views the ocean. She founded Dive Into Your Imagination (www.DiveIntoYourImagination.com), a multimedia company producing books, enhanced eBooks, educator guides, films, motivational art, and more. Annie was the photographer and filmmaker aboard SEAPLEX, courtesy of Project Kaisei and Samy's Camera. She is also a member of the Women Divers Hall of Fame. Visit her at www.AnnieCrawley.com.

THE ADDITIONAL IMAGES IN THIS BOOK ARE USED WITH THE PERMISSION OF: © Laura Westlund/Independent Picture Service, pp. 13, 22, 26; © Scripps Institution of Oceanography at UC San Diego, p. 18 (top); © Michele Hoffman Trotter, Microcosms p. 27; © Todd Strand/Independent Picture Service, p. 38; AP Photo/U.S. Navy, Jay C. Pugh, p. 39.

Main body text set in Serifa Std Light 13/18. Typeface provided by Adobe Systems.